26.25

DEC 10 2014

Published in 2014 by The Rosen Publishing Group, Inc.
29 East 21st Street, New York, NY 10010

Photo Credits: **KEY** tl=top left; tc=top center; tr=top right; cl=center left; c=center; cr=center right; b=bottom; bl=bottom left; bc=bottom center; br=bottom right; bg=background

CBT = Corbis; GI = Getty Images; iS = istockphoto.com; PDCD = PhotoDisc; SH = Shutterstock; TF = Topfoto

8bc GI; **8–9**bg GI; **9**bc, br, cr, tc SH; **12**b TF; **12–13**tc TF; **14**tl iS; **17**tl PDCD; cl SH; **22**bl, c SH; **22–23**tc GI; **25**cr CBT; **26**bl CBT; br SH; **27**br SH; **28**br iS; **29**c GI; bl, br iS; tr TF

All illustrations copyright Weldon Owen Pty Ltd, except **11**c, cl; **14**bl; **14–15**bc; **16**cb, cl; **17**br, cr; **20**br, tl; **22**cl; **23**br; **26**tl; **27**cl, cr Magic Group

Weldon Owen Pty Ltd
Managing Director: Kay Scarlett
Creative Director: Sue Burk
Publisher: Helen Bateman
Senior Vice President, International Sales: Stuart Laurence
Vice President Sales North America: Ellen Towell
Administration Manager, International Sales: Kristine Ravn

Library of Congress Cataloging-in-Publication Data

Close, Edward.
 Endangered animals / by Edward Close.
    pages cm. — (Discovery education: Habitats)
 Includes index.
 ISBN 978-1-4777-1325-9 (library binding) — ISBN 978-1-4777-1485-0 (paperback) —
ISBN 978-1-4777-1486-7 (6-pack)
1. Rare animals—Ecology—Juvenile literature. 2. Endangered species—Juvenile literature.
3. Endangered ecosystems—Juvenile literature. 4. Habitat (Ecology)—Juvenile literature.
5. Environmental degradation—Juvenile literature. 6. Habitat conservation—Juvenile literature. I.
Title.
 QL83.C55 2014
 591.68—dc23

                              2012043619

Manufactured in the United States of America

CPSIA Compliance Information: Batch #S13PK3: For Further Information contact Rosen Publishing, New York, New York at 1-800-237-9932

HABITATS

ENDANGERED ANIMALS

EDWARD CLOSE

PowerKiDS press.

New York

Contents

Sharing the Same World

The activities of humans have endangered many animal species around the world. An endangered species is a group of organisms that is at risk of becoming extinct. An extinct animal is one in which the last remaining member of the species is known, or presumed, to have died.

The rapid rise of the human population in the last 200 years has seen habitats that were once untouched being destroyed to make way for man-made structures. Rain forests and grasslands are vanishing, as are the animals that once lived there.

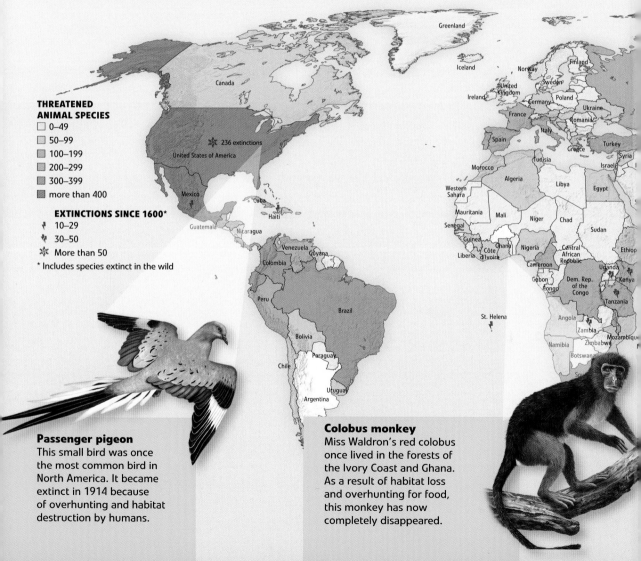

THREATENED ANIMAL SPECIES
- ☐ 0–49
- ☐ 50–99
- ☐ 100–199
- ☐ 200–299
- ☐ 300–399
- ☐ more than 400

EXTINCTIONS SINCE 1600*
- ⚑ 10–29
- ⚑ 30–50
- ❀ More than 50

* Includes species extinct in the wild

236 extinctions

Passenger pigeon
This small bird was once the most common bird in North America. It became extinct in 1914 because of overhunting and habitat destruction by humans.

Colobus monkey
Miss Waldron's red colobus once lived in the forests of the Ivory Coast and Ghana. As a result of habitat loss and overhunting for food, this monkey has now completely disappeared.

WILDLIFE IN DANGER

The International Union for Conservation of Nature publishes the Red List of Threatened Species. Around 8,000 animal species are endangered or threatened, including one in four mammal species and one in three amphibian species.

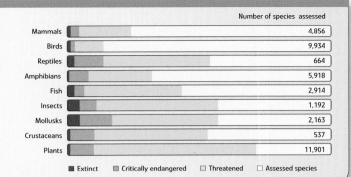

Number of species assessed

Mammals	4,856
Birds	9,934
Reptiles	664
Amphibians	5,918
Fish	2,914
Insects	1,192
Mollusks	2,163
Crustaceans	537
Plants	11,901

■ Extinct   ▨ Critically endangered   ▢ Threatened   ▢ Assessed species

Global warming

Experts believe that global warming is also responsible for the extinction of many animals. As weather conditions change, the habitats of many species may be destroyed. If the ice in polar regions continues to melt, species such as polar bears will not have enough territory to hunt for food.

Sea cow

Steller's sea cow was once abundant in the Pacific Ocean. Discovered by Europeans, this slow-moving mammal was hunted to extinction by 1768.

Dodo

This flightless bird was once found in large numbers on the island of Mauritius in the Indian Ocean. European sailors caused the bird's extinction in the mid-seventeenth century as a result of overhunting.

In the last 400 years, more than 600 species are known to have become extinct.

Habitat Destruction

From the early 1600s, as Europeans colonized other parts of the world, the human population exploded. To make room for this booming population, large areas of forests and wetlands were cleared. As a result, whole species were wiped out and had their habitats destroyed. Animals that once roamed free now faced extinction because of human destruction.

Disappearing forests

Deforestation is the clearing of natural forests through logging and burning. Many countries carry out logging and land clearing for economic gain. Deforestation causes the loss of habitat for thousands of animal species, and some scientists believe it may also be affecting Earth's climate.

At the current rate of deforestation, the entire world's rain forests could vanish within 100 years.

That's Amazing!

Tropical rain forests once covered 20 percent of all land area on Earth. Over the last 100 years, humans have cleared so much forest area that it now covers just 7 percent of the land.

WATER WORRIES

The overpopulation of many cities plays a huge role in shortages of fresh drinking water. People pump water from the ground for drinking, but if taken too quickly, groundwater will dry up.

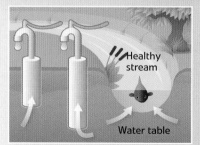

Sustainable water mining
Water has been pumped from under the ground for thousands of years. This is fine as long as people give the water source time to replenish.

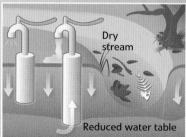

Drying up
When groundwater is pumped out faster than it can be replenished, the water level may drop and eventually dry up.

Causes of habitat loss

Many of the causes of habitat loss are influenced by humans. Practices such as land clearing, waste dumping, and mining, along with booming cities, all contribute to the loss of an animal's natural habitat.

Industrial pollution
This is pollution that is directly caused by factories. Many destroy habitats by polluting the air and dumping industrial waste.

Livestock grazing
The clearing of land by farmers for livestock grazing is a major cause of habitat loss. Forests are destroyed to make way for grass for livestock.

Mining
Improperly managed mines can destroy ecosystems and pollute waterways, degrading habitats in the process.

Urban sprawl
The growing population in cities causes habitat loss as more and more buildings are constructed in areas that were previously inhabited by animal species.

Animals in Danger

Habitat loss has been responsible for endangering many animal species around the globe and will remain a threat as the world's population continues to grow. Habitat loss occurs when an animal's environment is converted to other uses, such as building a housing development or clearing a forest for livestock grazing. Some species have an extremely limited habitat, so when this is destroyed, they have very little chance of surviving.

Orangutans
These amazing animals are disappearing rapidly because of logging and palm oil plantations. Sumatran orangutans are critically endangered, with only 6,500 currently alive.

Giant panda
This incredible mammal lives in the mountains of China. Because of habitat destruction, there are now fewer than 2,000 living in the wild.

Mountain gorilla
There are only 325 mountain gorillas left in the African wild, mainly due to the loss of rain forest habitat.

Sumatran tiger
This large cat is found only on the Indonesian island of Sumatra. The species is critically endangered due to extensive habitat loss.

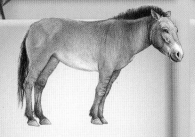

Przewalski's horse
This species from Mongolia became extinct in the wild in the 1960s. It was reintroduced into the wild in the 1980s after a successful breeding program.

Tomato frog
Native to Madagascar, this small amphibian is now endangered because of the large-scale deforestation of its habitat.

Leopard lizard
Found only in California, the blunt-nosed leopard lizard is listed as endangered because its habitat has been disturbed and destroyed.

European bison
This large beast was on the brink of extinction in the 1920s and is now a protected species. The bison's grazing range was reduced and this nearly wiped out the species.

Tree kangaroo
Goodfellow's tree kangaroo is a marsupial found in New Guinea. The species is endangered because its habitat is being destroyed for logging and agriculture.

Polar bear
The polar bear has become endangered due to the loss of its habitat from global warming. Earth's melting ice caps have seen large areas of the polar bear's habitat wiped out.

Hunting and Trading

The hunting of animals for food, trade, and recreation has been going on for thousands of years. Hunters used an animal's meat for food, bones for tools, and its fur, feathers, and leather for clothing. In recent years, hunting has changed from a means of survival in early civilization, to illegal poaching of species in Africa, and to trophy hunting in Europe and the Americas.

Japan has killed more than 8,000 minke whales in the Antarctic since the whaling moratorium was agreed to in 1986.

Whaling

Whales have long been hunted by many countries for their meat and oil. A variety of hunting methods have been used over time, including nets and harpoons. As whale populations began to drop significantly, whaling has been reduced to a very limited scale. It is the topic of strong debate by governments and environmental organizations.

Hunting bison

Bison have been hunted for thousands of years. Long before horses and weapons arrived in North America, the Plains Indians hunted the mammals on foot. The introduction of guns meant the bison were much easier to hunt. By 1880, the once-large herds had disappeared.

Russian fur trade

Between the sixteenth and eighteenth centuries, Russia became a major exporter of fur. The exploration of Siberia provided the Russians with various mammal species to hunt, including sea otters, walruses, and fur seals. By the second half of the nineteenth century, Russia was the world's largest supplier of fur.

Fact or Fiction?

The northern fur seal, found in the freezing waters of the North, was hunted to near extinction during the nineteenth century. It has now rebounded to a population of more than 1.3 million.

Animals Hunted

Sometimes people ignore laws protecting species and continue to hunt animals to the brink of extinction. Poaching is the illegal hunting, killing, or capturing of animals. Many endangered species are poached for their horn, ivory, teeth, bone, and fur, which can be traded on the black market for large sums of money. If people continue to hunt endangered animals, these species may disappear from our planet.

Snow leopards
These mighty beasts roam the mountains of Asia. They are now an endangered species because of poachers hunting them for their rare fur.

Some traditional Chinese medicines use parts of endangered species, such as rhinoceros horns and tiger claws, as ingredients.

African elephant
The African elephant once ranged the entire continent of Africa. The poaching of these animals for their ivory tusks has led to their endangerment.

WHALES

Whalers often used the bones and teeth of hunted sperm whales to make carvings, known as scrimshaw. Whalers would carve detailed drawings and patterns into the whalebone or teeth then color their designs with pigment.

Scrimshaw

The northern right whale is one of the rarest whales in the world.

Long-beaked echidna

This small animal is found in parts of Indonesia and Papua New Guinea. In recent years, the echidna's population has declined dramatically, as traditional hunters continue to kill the prized game animal.

Black rhinoceros

There are now fewer than 2,500 black rhinoceroses left in Africa. The major reason for their endangerment is poaching by hunters for their horns.

Scarlet macaws

These large, colorful birds are on the brink of extinction in Central and South America. Poachers continue to hunt and capture the species to sell them as pets on the black market.

Wiped Out by Strangers

As the human population continues to grow, some animals have been forced to share their habitats. Many people are unaware of the damage they are causing to an animal's habitat when they build a new house or clear land for a new highway. Species that once inhabited a forest are now often forced to find food from the trash humans leave behind.

Orange-bellied parrot
Due to competition from introduced birds, this colorful Australian parrot is listed as critically endangered, with fewer than 200 left in the wild.

That's Amazing!
Feral cats and dogs are from the same family as domestic cats and dogs but survive in the wild. They often roam in large packs and scavenge food from household trash and landfills.

Gila monster
This large, slow-moving lizard is native to the southwestern United States and northern Mexico. They are endangered by pets and by habitat loss from urban sprawl.

Ethiopian wolf
The Ethiopian wolf is the only wolf species living in Africa. Very few remain in the mountains of Ethiopia due to threats from domestic dogs and land clearing by farmers.

DOMESTIC PETS

In Australia, pet cats have been known to kill native kangaroos, possums, and birds, while some pet dogs have harmed wallabies, koalas, and bandicoots trying to survive in their natural environments.

Domestic dog and cat

Invading strangers

A major cause of endangered species is the introduction of uninvited species. These animals were originally released to help control pests, only to become much bigger problems themselves.

Cane toad

The large cane toad is native to Central and South America but has since been introduced to various islands in the Caribbean and Pacific. This amphibian breeds at a very fast rate and is now a major pest in some countries.

Common rat

This rodent, thought to be from China, now covers most continents. Rats carry diseases and are believed to be responsible for the bubonic plague.

Gray squirrel

The gray squirrel is a prolific breeder that was introduced to many countries across Europe and North America. As it is bigger and stronger, it has largely displaced the native red squirrel across Britain.

Red squirrel

The small red squirrel once inhabited large regions of Britain. Since the introduction of the larger gray squirrel to its habitat, it has been disappearing at a rapid rate.

European fox

This introduced species was brought to Australia from the Northern Hemisphere in the 1870s. It is now one of the most widely spread feral animals in Australia.

Pollution Problems

Waste dangers
Household waste that finds its way into oceans, lakes, and rivers can be mistaken by animals for food. Everyday items made of plastic, metal, and rubber can be deadly to animals if not disposed of properly.

We may see the dumping of trash as harmless, but it may be deadly to a hungry animal trying to survive. Poisons used on plants and pests may be swallowed by curious animals if disposed of improperly. Chemicals dumped into waterways will pollute drinking water and poison many animals. Oil spills in the ocean can significantly harm marine life. Many industrial pollutants will end up in our soil, air, and water, endangering many animal species.

Some animals that swallow chemicals will pass on traces of the pollutant when breeding. Before long, an entire species can be affected by the chemicals.

Air pollution
Industrial air pollution is a major environmental issue.

City sprawl
Urban sprawl results in increased traffic pollution and large amounts of trash from homes and buildings.

Saving our forests
The disappearance of rain forests is due to land clearing by humans. Forests are destroyed for farms, cities, and logging businesses.

Preventing air pollution
More industrialized countries now have tight controls on emissions polluting the air. The more countries that introduce these controls, the cleaner the environment for all.

CARBON DIOXIDE EMISSIONS

Many of the westernized countries are the worst carbon dioxide polluters in the world. Although the United States has only 5 percent of the global population, it produces over a quarter of the world's greenhouse gas emissions.

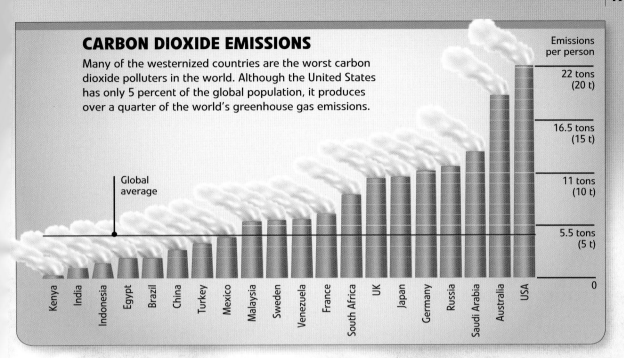

Emissions per person

22 tons (20 t)

16.5 tons (15 t)

11 tons (10 t)

5.5 tons (5 t)

0

Global average

Kenya | India | Indonesia | Egypt | Brazil | China | Turkey | Mexico | Malaysia | Sweden | Venezuela | France | South Africa | UK | Japan | Germany | Russia | Saudi Arabia | Australia | USA

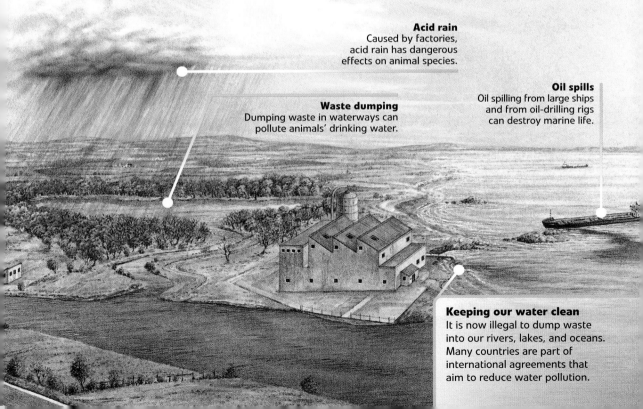

Acid rain
Caused by factories, acid rain has dangerous effects on animal species.

Oil spills
Oil spilling from large ships and from oil-drilling rigs can destroy marine life.

Waste dumping
Dumping waste in waterways can pollute animals' drinking water.

Keeping our water clean
It is now illegal to dump waste into our rivers, lakes, and oceans. Many countries are part of international agreements that aim to reduce water pollution.

Endangered by Pollution

Pollution has a large impact on the natural environment and the animals that inhabit it. More and more animals are dying because of our global pollution problems. Rubbish in our oceans can choke marine life, and oil spills can kill fish, seals, and birds. Chemicals such as pesticides are destroying entire natural habitats. Pollution from acid rain and mines that drains into streams and rivers has endangered many species in waterways around the world.

MANY-LEGGED FROG

Some scientists believe that frogs that develop deformities, such as extra legs, have been affected by chemical pollution. Chemicals are being dumped into waterways and swallowed by frogs that inhabit these areas.

Frog with deformity

Hawaiian monk seal
Many monk seals are dying after becoming entangled in ocean trash, such as nets and plastics. This has led to their population becoming endangered.

Coral reef
Many coral reefs around the world are being destroyed by pollution. Chemical runoff from farms and oil spills are threatening many reefs. Anchors from fishing and tourist boats are also damaging the beautiful coral.

Black-footed ferret

This small animal is an endangered mammal in North America. The ferret was a natural predator of the prairie dog. The large-scale killing of prairie dogs by humans has meant the ferret now has little food to survive.

Wolverine

The wolverine is found mainly in the Northern Hemisphere, particularly throughout Canada, Scandinavia, and Russia. It is endangered by hunters who kill it for its fur and through habitat destruction.

Gharial

The gharial is a crocodile-like reptile that is critically endangered. There are fewer than 200 breeding adults left in the world because of habitat loss.

Chinese paddlefish

These enormous fish once graced China's waterways. Human destruction of rivers and dams has affected breeding patterns of this species. No sightings have been made of the fish since 2003, with many people fearing they are already extinct.

Climate Change

Earth's climate is changing. Many scientists now agree the planet is getting warmer. This is leading to many changes in the environment. The steady rise in Earth's average temperature is known as global warming. The burning of fossil fuels, such as coal and oil, to produce energy pollutes Earth's atmosphere. In the last 100 years, Earth's temperature has increased by almost 2°F (1°C).

The greenhouse effect

The greenhouse effect is a natural process that helps keep the planet warm. Greenhouse gases, such as carbon dioxide and methane, trap the Sun's heat inside Earth's atmosphere. Over time, these gases have built up and the natural greenhouse effect has become much warmer.

Melting ice
As global warming causes temperatures on Earth to rise, ice melts in the polar regions. Ice shelves in the Arctic are estimated to have been shrinking by 7 percent each decade since the 1950s. This means that large amounts of water are flowing into the world's oceans. The oceans expand and sea levels rise.

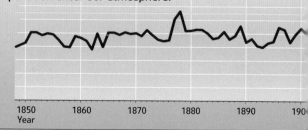

Solar energy
Some of the Sun's energy is absorbed by Earth's surface and warms it up.

WARMING UP

There has been a steady increase in Earth's average temperature since 1850. Temperatures are expected to get even warmer, as more greenhouse gases from pollution enter our atmosphere.

1850 1860 1870 1880 1890 190
Year

Deadly droughts
A drought can mean that there is not enough rain for farm crops to grow normally or for pastures to produce enough grass for livestock. Without rain, rivers and lakes can dry up and sometimes disappear completely. Without food and water, animals are unable to survive.

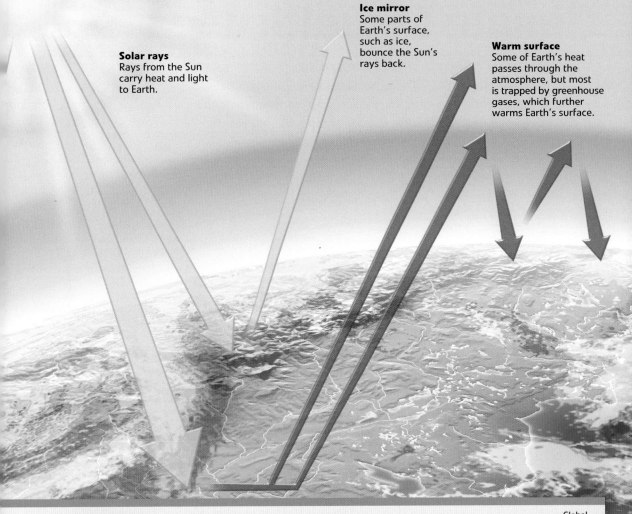

Solar rays
Rays from the Sun carry heat and light to Earth.

Ice mirror
Some parts of Earth's surface, such as ice, bounce the Sun's rays back.

Warm surface
Some of Earth's heat passes through the atmosphere, but most is trapped by greenhouse gases, which further warms Earth's surface.

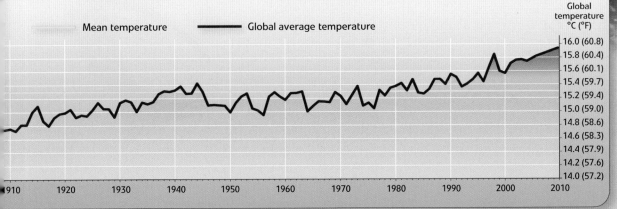

Mean temperature — Global average temperature

Global temperature °C (°F)

- 16.0 (60.8)
- 15.8 (60.4)
- 15.6 (60.1)
- 15.4 (59.7)
- 15.2 (59.4)
- 15.0 (59.0)
- 14.8 (58.6)
- 14.6 (58.3)
- 14.4 (57.9)
- 14.2 (57.6)
- 14.0 (57.2)

1910 1920 1930 1940 1950 1960 1970 1980 1990 2000 2010

Climate Casualties

Experts believe that climate change problems, such as warmer temperatures and more extreme weather, are adding to the endangerment of animal species on Earth. As the weather conditions change, the habitats of animals and plants may be destroyed. Some animals and plants may be able to adapt to new conditions, but others may not be able to survive an increase in temperature or find enough food, water, and shelter if their environment changes.

Apollo butterfly
The Apollo butterfly inhabits mountain meadows and pastures across Europe. Rising temperatures have allowed forest trees to grow higher up the mountains, blocking the precious sunlight this species needs to survive.

Pika
This small rabbit-like animal is at risk of becoming extinct because of global warming. As temperatures rise, the pika's habitat is no longer cold enough for its survival.

Arctic fox
There are only 150 arctic foxes still alive in mainland Europe. The melting Arctic ice has forced predators to compete for food, causing the foxes to become critically endangered.

Polar bear
With the rising temperatures in polar regions, the future of polar bears is uncertain. If the sea ice in the polar areas continues to melt, polar bears will not have enough territory to hunt for seals and fish.

Pacific hawksbill turtle
Warming oceans are causing coral reefs to die. This threatens the hawksbill turtle, as coral reefs are important food sources and habitats for the species.

Macaroni penguin
As the Antarctic continent heats up from global warming, the sea ice where penguins live is disappearing. Newborn penguins are being swept into the ocean and adult penguins are having difficulty finding food.

Golden toad
The extinct golden toad was once found in the rain forests of Costa Rica. This species died out in 1987 because of a fast-spreading disease caused by warmer temperatures.

Trout
As freshwater rivers and lakes warm up, fish that were once common in colder waters—such as trout and salmon—are becoming threatened.

Saving Endangered Species

An important way to help endangered animals survive is to protect their habitats through wilderness areas, nature reserves, and national parks. In these sanctuaries, they can live without interference from humans. It is also important to protect habitats outside reserves, such as on farms and along roadsides. People who live on farms need to be encouraged to keep patches of forest as wildlife habitats. Some environmental groups look after local nature reserves.

Species have been saved from extinction by captive-breeding programs. These include the black-footed ferret, California condor, and Przewalski's horse.

Captive-breeding programs
This is a method of breeding animals in a controlled environment when they cannot survive in the wild. The Andean condor matures late and reproduces slowly. It is being bred in captivity and released back into the wild.

Banning trade
Although some countries have banned the trade of threatened species, many others continue to allow it. Countries such as Canada continue to hunt polar bears, while poachers in Africa carry on trading ivory from elephants and rhinoceros horns.

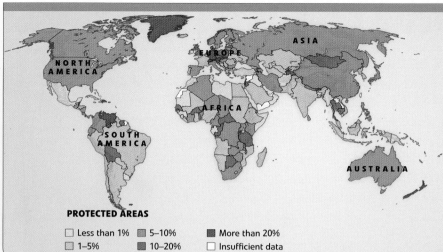

PROTECTED AREAS

The amount of land reserved for wildlife protection varies from country to country. Despite many regions being declared wildlife reserves, poachers, loggers, and developers continue to threaten animal species.

PROTECTED AREAS

- ☐ Less than 1%
- ☐ 1–5%
- ▨ 5–10%
- ▨ 10–20%
- ▪ More than 20%
- ☐ Insufficient data

Wildlife corridors

Creating habitat corridors for wildlife to connect between nature reserves will encourage breeding and help with survival. Wildlife corridors are very important for larger species, such as giant pandas, which graze over large areas.

Okapi Wildlife Reserve

This reserve in the Democratic Republic of Congo was once threatened by deforestation, farming, and mining. It was listed as a World Heritage site in 1997 and is home to one-sixth of the world's okapi population.

Jaguar recovery programs

In the United States, a recovery plan for jaguars was set out to designate critical habitat for this endangered species. These refuges will help protect the jaguars from hunters and prevent loggers from destroying their remaining habitat.

How Can We Help?

One way we can help save our endangered species is by addressing climate change. Reducing the levels of carbon dioxide and other greenhouse gases created by humans is the best way to slow down global warming. Reducing waste and recycling materials help tackle climate change because less energy is used to create new products. People are starting to use energy that causes much less pollution, such as wind or solar power. This is sometimes called clean, or green, energy.

The largest wind turbines in the world can generate enough energy to power a small town.

Renewable wind power
Wind power is the process of converting wind energy into electricity by using wind turbines. Wind makes the large rotors turn, which gives power to a generator. This power is then converted to electricity.

Solar panels
Solar power is a clean and renewable source of energy. Cells in solar panels collect the Sun's rays and convert them into electricity. Once, solar panels could be placed only on roofs, but today whole buildings can be clad in solar panels.

USA
28 tons (25 t) per person, per year

The goal
3.3 tons (3 t) per person, per year

Planting trees
The replanting of native trees allows native forest to gradually regenerate. This is one way to restore the natural habitat of many species and encourage native animals to return. Trees also reduce the amount of carbon dioxide in the atmosphere.

Africa
1 ton (0.9 t) per person, per year

Reducing carbon footprint
A carbon footprint is the total amount of greenhouse gases produced by everything you do. It measures how the activities we perform impact on the environment. The average carbon footprint in the United States is 28 times that of the average footprint in Africa.

UK
12.7 tons (11.5 t) per person, per year

Recycling waste
Instead of being dumped, many used materials can be recycled. The old items are collected, processed, and made into new products. Recycling saves energy and raw materials.

Plastic bags
Billions of plastic bags are thrown away each year. Many are dumped in the ocean and become a danger to wildlife. Some towns have banned free plastic shopping bags.

Glossary

acid rain (A-sud RAYN)
Rain containing chemicals that form in the atmosphere when industrial gas emissions combine with water.

amphibian
(am-FIH-bee-un) A cold-blooded vertebrate that usually lives on land, but breeds in water.

black market
(BLAK MAHR-ket) An illegal market in which goods such as rare furs, precious stones, and weapons are bought and sold.

chemical runoff
(KEH-mih-kul RUN-of) The overflow of surplus liquid containing chemicals such as fertilizers and pesticides, which is carried into rivers, lakes, and oceans.

climate change
(KLY-mut CHAYNG) Changes in Earth's climate, especially those produced by global warming.

deforestation
(dee-for-uh-STAY-shun) The removal of forest trees, often as a result of human activities such as logging.

deformity
(dih-FOR-muh-tee) A part of the body that has developed in a misshapen or malformed way, sometimes as a result of environmental pollution.

domestic pets
(duh-MES-tik PETS) Household pets, such as cats or dogs, which are kept as companions for the family.

drought (DROWT)
An extended period of lower than average rainfall, usually combined with extremely warm temperatures.

ecosystem
(EE-koh-sis-tem) A community of organisms, including plants and animals, all living together in their environment.

endangered
(in-DAYN-jerd) Describes a species population that is so small it is in danger of becoming extinct.

environment
(en-VY-ern-ment) All the surroundings and conditions that affect the growth and health of all living things within an area.

extinct (ik-STINGKT)
Describes an entire species that has completely died out and is no longer in existence.

fossil fuels (FO-sul FYOOL)
Fuels formed by fossilized natural resources, including petroleum oil, coal, and natural gas.

global warming
(GLOH-bul WAWRM-ing) An increase in the average temperature of Earth's atmosphere.

grasslands (GRAS-landz)
Large regions of land where grass or grasslike plants grow and are the dominant form of vegetation.

greenhouse gases
(GREEN-hows GAS-ez)
Gases in Earth's atmosphere, such as carbon dioxide and methane, which contribute to the greenhouse effect.

habitat (HA-buh-tat)
The type of environment where animals and plants live.

household waste
(HOWS-hold WAYST)
The trash that is produced in the home, such as food scraps, packaging, and papers.

industrial pollutants
(in-DUS-tree-ul puh-LOO-tantz) Harmful products from large industrial companies, including chemical waste and toxic emissions.

land clearing
(LAND KLEER-ing) The removal of native trees and vegetation for farming purposes or because of urban sprawl.

livestock grazing
(LYV-stok GRAYZ-ing) The feeding and roaming of animal species in a particular region.

logging (LOG-ing) The process of cutting down forest trees for timber or land clearing.

mammal (MA-mul) Any warm-blooded, air-breathing vertebrate whose skin is more or less covered with hair or fur.

marsupial
(mahr-SOO-pee-ul) A type of mammal. The female has a pouch in which young live and feed after birth.

native (NAY-tiv) Describes plants and animals that are indigenous to a particular geographic area.

organism
(OR-guh-nih-zum) A living thing that has, or can develop, the ability to act or function independently.

overhunting
(OH-ver-hunt-ing) The hunting of species of animals to the extent that they become endangered or extinct.

poaching (POHCH-ing) The illegal hunting, fishing, trapping, or eating of wild plants or animals.

polar region
(POH-lur REE-jun) The area near the North and South Poles on Earth.

population
(pop-yoo-LAY-shun) A group of organisms of the same species inhabiting a given area.

rain forest (RAYN FOR-est) A large area of trees and other plants characterized by high rainfall and home to many animal species.

regenerate
(rih-JEH-neh-rayt) To regrow, replenish, and return to its natural state.

reptile (REP-tyl) One of a group of cold-blooded animals with a backbone including snakes, turtles, lizards, and alligators.

solar energy
(SOH-ler EH-nur-jee) Energy from the sun that is trapped by solar panels and converted into thermal or electrical energy.

species (SPEE-sheez) A group of animals or plants that share many common characteristics.

urban sprawl
(UR-bun SPROL) The spreading outward of a city and its suburbs to its outskirts to low-density and rural areas of land that were previously untouched by humans.

whaling (HWAY-ling) The hunting of whales mainly for meat and oil.

wildlife corridor
(WYLD-lyf KOR-uh-dur) An area of habitat connecting wildlife populations separated by human activities. It allows animals to move safely from region to region.

Index

A
acid rain 19, 20
amphibians 7, 11, 17
Apollo butterflies 24

B
bison 11, 13, 14
bubonic plague 17

C
carbon dioxide 22, 28, 29
Chinese paddlefish 21
coral reef 20, 25

D
deforestation 8, 11, 27
deformities 20
drought 22

E
echidnas 15
ecosystem 9
elephants 14, 26

F
fossil fuels 22
foxes 17, 24
fur trade 13

G
giant pandas 11, 27
global warming 7, 11, 22, 24,
        25, 28
gorillas 11
grasslands 6
greenhouse effect 22, 23
greenhouse gas 22, 23, 28, 29

I
ivory 14, 26

L
leopards 14
lizards 11, 16
logging 8, 10, 11

M
macaws 11, 15
mammals 7, 13, 21

O
Okapi Wildlife Reserve 27
orangutans 10
overpopulation 8

P
palm oil plantation 10
parrots 16
penguins 25

pesticides 20
poaching 12, 14, 15
polar bears 7, 11, 24, 26
polar region 7, 22, 24

R
rain forest 6, 8, 18, 25
rhinoceroses 14, 15
rodents 17

S
seals 13, 20, 24
solar energy 22
squirrels 16, 17

T
tigers 11
toads 17, 25
trout 25

W
waste dumping 9, 19
water mining 8
wetlands 8
whaling 12
wind power 28
wolves 16
wolverines 21

Websites

Due to the changing nature of Internet links, PowerKids Press has developed an online list of websites related to the subject of this book. This site is updated regularly. Please use this link to access the list:
www.powerkidslinks.com/disc/endan/